An Abundance of You

Varsha Vinod

Presentation by *BookLeaf Publishing*

Web: www.bookleafpub.com

E-mail: info@bookleafpub.com

ISBN: 9789357442268

First edition 2023

To Amma, Achan, & Atta, for letting me do every crazy thing that I feel compelled to do.

To Jaime, for showing me that nothing is impossible

To Achamma, Ammamma, Muthachan, for unconditional love and perspective

PREFACE

Ideas that came about in restless dreams or fleeting moments; deep, ornate, feelings indescribable by singular words.

My timer was set for 25 minutes,

but over 50 have passed

My planner has only 10 lines for each day
but I have far too many tasks.

I used to be happy when I kept busy
I used to be somebody else

but it seems life has pit every challenge against me
and this time, I'm not doing too well.

But it's funny because when I start to feel the despair
it seems all I have to do

is scroll back a bit through my camera roll
and find that picture of you.

Achan and I wear AirPods
when we run

I am right (R) and he is left (L)
I have to hound him some,
but he is keeping up

When I am away, I wear both AirPods when I run
He is always whispering in my left ear
"Kanna, you were my lucky charm"

Studio

The same mid tone tables with indented
scribbles
see us every day of the week but one
Pulling faces in confusion and wrinkling
eyebrows in distrust
We bicker and curse, then we douse each other
in love
Saying each others' work is something special
for the world to see
And I don't mean to be cheesy but
it is and it will be
(and not just to me)
You tell me about how you were raised different
and the books your dad likes to read
and we make plans for all the arthouse movies
it seems like we'll never see
I say you should come to Chicago
and you say that you will someday,
that we'd both go to Singapore this very second
if it wasn't so damn far away
You seem to just work and rework
brown eyes glued to the glass
I want to tell you to stop trying so hard,
you have real work after class
You've tried to explain it all to your parents

but of course they'll never understand
So I want to drive the 40 minutes,
"Admitting one's wrongs doesn't make any less
of a man."
But instead I stay here and offer a smile
because even though we only whine,
I revel in the fact that we were all brought
together,
here, at this moment in time.

Feminine Rage

5

Give me your candles; give me your light
Flakes of wax pressed between my fingers
Your stature short and mighty eyes
And you hold all my wilt and anger

Give me your eyes; yours bore into mine
And give me your hollow palms too
Nourish my skin with that incense, with flame
And follow my bruised lips, anew

I love you to Mercury and back
The moon could not be far enough
Through disbelief and shaky frames
Am I the vessel of your love?

Guide me forward, into the night
Show me your feminine rage
Show me once more where I come from
Light me the path with your sage

Melody

I want you to study every inch of me the way
that you study at work
So meticulously, gingerly, leaving no stone
unturned

I want you to touch me the way that you handle
the keys
So delicately, lovingly, touching every part of
me

I want every inch of personal space between us
to seize to exist
Skin to connect with skin; a union sealed with a
kiss

I watched those hands for far too long, I want to
know how they feel
I want to sit on the beach with soft music, with
your arms wrapped all around me

You are the melody I wish that I wrote
Painstakingly; every perfect note

You are the poetry I wish that I spoke
Rhythmic, true, and vulnerable

You are the silence in between of my teeth
And the stuttering and the powerless speak

You are the dysfunction and the making me
weak
You are the passion I wish I could keep

Envy of Contentment

Your sweet saccharine smile
Seeps into my bones
And I just wish you didn't feel
So much like home

Memory

Sweet child of lavish desires
Don't cry as memory fades
As time beckons your unfastened fire
This feeling will too wash away

Skin does not peel in musical sheets
Away with the ferocious wind
Love too can mellow; I promise it keeps
Into and after the end

Sweet child of lavish desires
Your mind has dissembled you well
Don't fear for the future of your little brother
His essence is his own to dwell

Age does not sweep you nor rob you of youth
Time is not yours to abhor
Avail yourself of its exuberant truths
Evanescent but pure

Sweet child of lavish desires
Fear not the clock's stern beat
On adventure's coattails, continue to tire
Forever is still at your feet.

I saw a car junkyard up close for the first time the other day

The train rumbled beneath me passing meters
and meters of the broken bodies of cars.

Some cars are beaten up to the bone,
utterly obliterated hollowed out homes of once
living, breathing, laughing beings.
Almost comically deformed show pieces.
You could hardly call them vehicles in their
current state.

And some looked…perfectly fine barring the
dust accumulating on the windows
Some not safe for work phrases or couples'
initials on display on now gray glass
Maybe there were some internal issues.

But they all ended up here regardless.
I guess sometimes damage is visible from the
outside and sometimes it is not.
I guess damage is damage nonetheless.

Say No

You're not like a fire
You're not like a show
You're not like (anything)
I've ever known

but you can call my name
And I'll always answer
Because to you,
my heart cannot say no

And you build me up
Piece by piece, not a tremble
Your fleece around me
Safe and warm

Because into you, I can fall
With no hesitation
You're unlike (anything)
I've ever known

Designer Smile

What came from my fingertips
Is no longer mine
The words that once helped me
Now blur the lines
And I learn that I'm wrong every single time
No more black ties
Ink bleeds from my eyes
This is my designer smile

Indifference

My heart floods with implacable feeling
The dam of my ribs broken in
Tsunami of intensity
I can't make the wretched climb again

I wander secluded cliffside scenes
All this sensation having nowhere to go
I ache for a mere second of tranquility
Indifference is a thing I will never know

I once received a piece of embroidery advice

It's okay if you make a mistake because when you mess up, you can just remove the needle and try each stroke again. A hole lingers at first, but you can just keep going. Watch the material stretch around it, and it slowly disappears.

There are two types of people in this world

Those who slow down at yellow lights and those
who speed up
You will always be the latter
You wade through life with patience and poise
And take what comes your way
Yet you never slam the brake
When people don't do the same
You know you'll soon get the green
So "what's the rush?" you say
If I could, I'd shotgun life
with you every day

How do you know you love me?

I know because you drive me utterly insane,
Yet when someone speaks badly of you I can't
help but defend your name

I know because every time I see that you're late,
I curse at the sky until I see your face

I know because every haircut or change
Changes nothing; to me you're simply the same

I know because it won't matter what you say,
I know you, and your eyes can show me the
way.

Two Windmills Turn in Unison; One Falls out of Rhythm

On the bittersweet drive through Indiana
To drop brother off at college
I peer out of the backseat window
And the sky is fragmented by white
windmills tower to the sky
And off in the distance
Two stand alone
turning and turning in unison
Until the wind falters for a split second

Finding Yourself

You say you are finding yourself.
I ask you where you think you might have lost
yourself.
Under the couch? In the secret zipper of your
backpack?
Where did you last see yourself?
In your high school senior photo? The videos of
you laughing at the beach?
When did you lose yourself?
When you were drawing in the study? Or when
you drew conclusions as a child? When opinions
penetrated a little deeper than they were
supposed to?
Or when you realized you couldn't smile the
same
You realize you did not lose yourself.
Underneath yesterday's laundry and mummy's
screams,
Underneath crayon sets and "stupid dreams"
Think about when you laughed so hard the ice
cream fell out of your mouth
Think about every time you cried in the bathtub
Think about when he got bullied, and you stood
up

Think about the grit in your heart, next to all the love
There, underneath everything else, you will find yourself.

Void

One deep void blemishes the earth
And approaching it's monstrous temptation
is the boy with the belt of lightning
and anger and ancient frustration

Every stride is a reach for somewhere
His past has been thrust far behind
Denting the sandstone are his rigid boots
Tainted footprints behind which, are mine

I follow far behind him
But he's fixated on his track
Proving himself of the already proven
He looks forward but never back

I call for him to turn around
But cries fall on deaf ears
His electric fingers tremble
He's been chasing her for years

He peers into the blackness
Teeth clenched and pride upheld
My tears drip onto sandstone
He looks for her; He sees himself

One deep void blemishes the earth
And in front of it he stands
Looking forward but never back
He holds the lightning in his hands.

An Abundance of You

I told you once I liked dinosaurs
Politics, language, and film too
And you told me once you liked what I liked
And that you loved to learn something new

I told you I read about the Indus Valley
What that was, you didn't have a clue
But you told me you loved to hear me talk
And asked me what I think of you

How is it that one can spend 8 hours with
someone
and still feel as if it wasn't enough?
How can it be that we talked the full time,
yet there's so much I forgot to bring up?

And usually I'm full of things to say
I could give stats and evidence too
I can tell you the exact reasons why
we think or act like we do

But my mind now runs blank; don't know what
to do
I scour through my mind, searching for context
clues

But all I can find up there is
An abundance of you

23

"Don't take it so personally"

But I am a person!
I don't have the flesh and bones of a fish,
the brain of a computer,
or the teeth and nails of a mannequin,
plastic or vinyl for sonic waves to just ricochet
No magic erasers to leave me scotch-free

So treat me like a person!
Take care of my hair,
braiding it before my sleep
String words through my ears
and hang me right up,
instead of rubbing your stones against me

(And hoping
I won't take it personally)

Tides

25

No matter how long it takes you to draw a
picture in the sand, the waves wash it away just
the same. Don't resist the tides of nature, and let
your past and future wash away.

Love like You

"We don't know what it's like to love as much as
you,
But we do love that you love as much as you do"

www.ingramcontent.com/pod-product-compliance
Lightning Source LLC
LaVergne TN
LVHW021339200726
843509LV00014B/2579